# Helsinki

*by*
Oscar Valdes

Copyright © 2018 by Oscar Valdes

All rights reserved. No part of this publication may be reproduced, distributed or transmitted in any form or by any means, including photocopying, recording, digital scanning or other electronic or mechanical methods, without the prior written permission of the publisher, except in the case of brief quotations embodied in critical reviews and certain other noncommercial uses permitted by copyright law.

This book is a production of Editorial Madruga,
P.O. Box 78, Pasadena, CA 91102

You may visit the author online at oscarvaldes.net.

Library of Congress Control Number: 2018910697

Published 2018
Printed in the United States of America
Print ISBN: 978-1-7327788-0-1
E ISBN: 978-1-7327788-1-8

Cover and interior design by Ann Valdés

*For my daughter.*

Dear Mr. Trump,

There's still time, dear sir,
It's not too late,
for you to spark the dialogue
that will unleash the creativity
now locked in bitter acrimony.
Still time, dear sir,
not too late,
for you to govern from the center
and marshal the forces of the nation.

Nature loves diversity.
It experiments ceaselessly with difference,
Giving to each something unique,
And challenging us with each gift
To join forces in pursuit of a common,
Higher,
And transcendent good.

7/16/18

Helsinki

Early in the day
**Trump tweets** — Our relationship with Russia has NEVER been worse thanks to many years of U.S. foolishness and stupidity and now, the Rigged Witch Hunt!

(the 'rigged witch hunt' is the President's term for the Mueller probe – A US Dept of Justice investigation assigned with the task of finding evidence of Russia's interference in the 2016 election and if any obstruction by the Trump administration. It has been in progress since May 2017)

At the press conference following Trump and Putin's meeting:

**Reporter (to President Trump)** —... Do you hold Russia at all accountable for anything in particular? And if so, what would you — what would you consider them — that they are responsible for?

**Trump** — Yes I do. I hold both countries responsible. I think that the United States has been foolish. I think we've all been foolish. We should've had this dialogue a long time ago; a long time, frankly, before I got to office. And I think we're all to blame. I think that the United States now has stepped forward along with Russia, and we're getting together and we have a chance to do some great things, whether it's nuclear proliferation in terms of stopping — you have to do it, ultimately that's probably the most important thing that we could be working on. But I do feel that we have both made some mistakes. I think that the — the probe is a disaster for our country. I think it's kept us apart, it's kept us separated. There was no collusion at all…

Moments later, in response to a separate question, Vladimir Putin denies having anything to do with the election interference of 2016.

**Reporter Jonathan Lemire, then asks President Trump** — … Every US Intelligence has concluded that Russia did (interfere). Who do you believe?
Would you now, with the whole world watching, tell President Putin, would you denounce what happened in 2016, and would you warn him to never do it again.

**Trump** — … my people came to me, Dan Coats came to me and others, they said they think it's Russia… I have President Putin… he just said it's not Russia. I will say this… I don't see any reason why it would be… I have confidence in both parties…
I have great confidence in my intelligence people… but I will tell you that President Putin was extremely strong and powerful in his denial today.

Questions and answers as reported by the New York Times and the Washington Post.

The next day. The White House.

In response to criticism that he went easy on Putin, Trump says,

"The sentence should have been 'I don't see any reason why it wouldn't be Russia', sort of a double negative. So you can put that in and that probably clarifies things pretty good."

# 1

Donald and Melania are sitting in their White House suite. At the table.

**Melania** — What happened?
**Donald** — Nothing. The press, as usual, is making much too much of it.
**Melania** — I was watching. I felt like I had been punched in the stomach.
**Donald** — Why?
**Melania** — Because in front of Putin, of all people, you devalue our intelligence services.
**Donald** — Didn't I come right back and correct myself?
**Melania** — 'I don't see any reason why it wouldn't be Russia. Sort of a double negative,' you add casually. Sorry. That won't do.
And then you go right back into your old rant that there was no collusion.
**Donald** — Rant?
**Melania** — What else am I supposed to call it?

He gets up and walks over to the window.

**Donald** — It was a bad moment, I'll agree.
**Melania** — It is the beginning of the end.

He crosses his arms as he looks out into the evening light.

**Melania** — That video clip will haunt you for the rest of your life.
**Donald** — Right. And you see me shaking in my boots,

don't you?
**Melania** — All the worse.

She rises and steps over to join him.

**Donald** — I thought you believed me when I said there was no collusion.
**Melania** — Still do. But your contempt for the Mueller investigation undermines your case.
And you've been stuck in that position.
**Donald** — It's all politics. They're after my head and I won't hand it over.
**Melania** — If you're innocent what's there to fear?
**Donald** — You're being naïve. They have a way of setting up traps.

They look at each other.

**Melania** — Putin, who annexed the Crimea and invaded the Ukraine, Putin, whose people shot down the Malaysian airliner…
**Donald** — It didn't happen on my watch.
**Melania** — You think he's holding back because of you?
**Donald** — He hasn't annexed more territory.
**Melania** — Not yet.

She shakes her head, disapprovingly.

**Melania** — As President, you stand for something far larger than yourself…
**Donald** — It'll blow over, like everything else.
**Melania** — Not this. In Helsinki, you failed.

He crosses his arms.

**Donald** — You really think this is all that damaging?
**Melania** — It is the beginning of the end.
**Donald** — Well, then, my lady, it will give me great pleasure to prove you wrong.
**Melania** — Do you really not believe that Russian hackers interfered with the election?
**Donald** — They set up some fake accounts but their impact didn't affect the outcome.
**Melania** — The electoral votes of three states where you won by less than 80 thousand votes made the difference.
**Donald** — You cannot prove that those fake accounts changed their minds.
**Melania** — You cannot disprove it, either.
**Donald** — The point is then moot.
**Melania** — How could that large scale operation go on in Russia without Putin's consent?
**Donald** — There's always rogue operators.
**Melania** — Rogue operators?
**Donald** — Yes, of course. Look, I don't know everything that goes on in this country.

She looks at him, incredulous.

**Melania** — You don't think Putin is a dictator, with complete control of his country?
**Donald** — There are different kinds of dictators, some likeable and some not. Russians like Putin. For the most part.
**Melania** — And you do too.
**Donald** — Do I like Putin? Personally? Yes. I do. What's wrong with that?
**Melania** — What's wrong with that is that when you were

elected President you became the moral beacon of the nation, and when you like Putin you're letting him off the hook.

**Donald** — I said I like him personally, that does not mean I approve of his actions.

**Melania** — But you believe his denials. That's where the liking him comes in.

**Donald** — It's tactical. My greater aim is to negotiate with him, to keep world peace. And to do that I need to have a common bond.

**Melania** — You're giving him a free pass.

**Donald (angrily)** — I'm not giving him a free pass!

**Melania** — That's not what the clip showed. It showed you fooling yourself, and because you're our President, you're fooling us too.

He turns and takes a few steps into the room.

**Donald** — Where does it say that when I became president I became the moral beacon of the nation?

**Melania** — It's implicit.

**Donald** — I am a deal maker. I was elected to solve problems, and that's what I'm doing. I was elected to put more money in peoples' pockets, to cut back on regulations, to cut back taxes. I was elected to raise tariffs so I can protect the wellbeing of my fellow Americans. I was elected to stanch the flow of immigrants into this country because we have enough already and they're taking advantage of us. I was elected to make America great again. To do that, I have to deal with a lot of folks. And it helps if you like them. It's easier to do business and you get more done.

Anyway, the voters must've been fed up with moral beacons that they chose me.

**Melania** — They are already regretting it.
**Donald** — Really? Well, here's my answer to you. I'm going to get reelected in 2020. I know that. I already have a lot of money coming in in political contributions and there's no one — no one — who will come even close to matching my campaign treasure. Money talks.
**Melania** — Put another way... Money Trumps Morality.
**Doanld (chuckling)** — I live in the real world, Melania, not a purity bubble. I may not have been moral, according to you, but I have been successful.
**Melania** — Will Vladimir be in the stands cheering you on when you get reelected?
**Doanld** — I hadn't thought of that but now that you mention it, I just might invite him.

He returns to the window and stands next to her.

**Melania** — Does viewing the video clip of Helsinki not make you sick?
**Donald** — It does not. I'm not squeamish.
**Melania** — Then, there's something wrong with you. Deeply wrong.
**Donald** — Have you not known that for a while?

She looks at him.

**Melania** — I have.
**Donald** — And still you stayed.
**Melania** — Yes.
**Donald** — You've enjoyed the accommodations?
**Melania** — I suppose.
**Donald** — Having my child?
**Melania (testily)** — Our child.

**Donald** — Enjoyed being in the limelight?
**Melania** — Nothing of what you're saying discredits me.
**Donald** — If you think I'm morally corrupt, then you are too.
**Melania** — You're in such a rush to put me down, aren't you?
But you overlook that I've been willing to work with you.
You, who unlike me, does not view marriage as a commitment to improving each other, no matter what the circumstances, known and unknown.

She walks off a few paces, then turns to face him again.

Have I enjoyed the trappings of power? I have.
But I am not cheering you on, am I?
No, I am taking you to task as I should.
As usual, though, you have trouble sorting out your personal discomfort.

He lowers his head as he joins his hands in front of him.

**Donald** — We're cut from the same cloth, dear. And we might as well have fun with it.

She smiles wryly at him.

**Melania** — There's a difference.
**Donald** — What would that be?
**Melania** — I'm going to do something about it.

He looks at her distrustfully.

**Melania** — That video clip that did not make you sick but

did me and millions of Americans, showed you desperately wanting to be liked by Putin, and that goes well beyond allowing oneself to like someone because it might help transact business. What the clip showed was that, for some reason, you *need* to be liked by Putin.
**Donald (irritated)** — I don't need to be liked by Putin!
**Melania** — Go back and watch the clip.

He closes his eyes and quiet follows.

**Donald** — You are wrong. Very wrong.

He goes back into the room and sits at the table. He leans forward, rubbing his face, then sits back.

**Donald** — I would never betray my country.
**Melania** — I know you wouldn't. But Neville Chamberlain, in 1938, didn't set out to betray England when he let Hitler talk him into trading a part of Czechoslovakia for a promise of peace.

She returns to the table to join him. She takes a seat.

**Donald** — Why has there not been more of an uproar about what the clip showed?
**Melania** — There has been an uproar, you're just growing deaf to public outcries. You prefer to listen to Fox News and talk to their commentators who tell you what you want to hear. And so, slowly, you've been slipping into a cocoon that others are too eager to provide. You want a glass of cider?

He nods.

She goes in the closet and gets a bottle of cider and some low calorie crackers. She opens the bottle and serves the crackers. He pours the cider.

**Donald** — You want to have sex?
**Melania** — No.
**Donald** — Why not?
**Melania** — It would be a distraction.

He sips from his glass.

**Donald** — Did you want to talk about Stormy Daniels?
**Melania** — We'll get to that. We need to talk about your legitimacy as President.
**Donald** — My legitimacy?
**Melania** — Yes. We have reason to question it.
**Donald** — There's no way of proving that the interference made a difference…. it's a witch hunt.

She picks up her glass and holds it high up.

**Melania** — 'please, carry on, folks, as fast as you can, let's clear the air. Do make haste, for the sake of the country, for there are many other things that need our attention and are being neglected'.
(then turning to Donald)
Will you ever be able to say that about the Mueller probe?

He shrugs dismissively.

**Donald** — We should talk about Stormy.
**Melania** — Stormy can wait. And Karen… and whoever else.

**Donald** — Melania… I am a flawed man and you've known it all along.
And dammit, I am innocent! I did not collude with Putin!
**Melania** — Then start acting like it!

They say nothing for a moment.

**Melania** — Openly criticizing staunch allies like Theresa May and Angela Merkel is harmful… and so is starting a needless trade war.

**Donald** — I need my war.
**Melania** — Sure you do… and you do to distract us from addressing your legitimacy.
Bluster and blarney.

He rises and walks off a few paces.

**Donald** — Mueller will try and set me up.
**Melania** — You just do not trust our institutions, do you?
**Donald** — Maybe I don't.
**Melania** — And you do not trust yourself with Putin.

He turns around.

**Melania** — If you had trusted yourself, when the reporter asked the pointed question about Russian interference, you would've calmly turned to Putin, looked him in the eye, and said, 'my intelligence services have established that there was interference from your nation in our elections, and it is them whom I believe.'

He shakes his head in disagreement.

**Melania** — And when the reporter pressed you for an answer to his second question, demanding you publicly warn Putin never to do it again, you could simply have replied, 'the time and place for that is my prerogative, I make my choices, thank you, next question', and you could've done so with dignity because with your first answer you had taken the reins.

He turns and heads back to stand by the window, looking out.

**Melania** — But who knows what you said to him when you met in private, with only the translators.

They say nothing for a moment.

**Melania** — It's a problem, Dee… a big problem. If you don't trust yourself, then why should we trust you?

He crosses to the foot of the bed where his jacket lies, picks it up and walks toward the door.

**Donald** — I'm going for a walk. Need to clear my head.

He exits.

# 2

Donald strolls by himself in the White House lawn. It's already dark. After a while he goes back inside and into the Oval Office. He sits at his desk.

**Donald** — I could've been more forceful. Melania's right. Why wasn't I? That's my ghosts coming back to haunt me. Moral beacon, she says? Hunh. How do you do that? There's no way in hell that I'll ever fill those shoes. I don't see it.
I can make us some money, that I can do, but moral beacon?

He pauses.

I think I can win this trade war, I'm pretty sure about that. And I'm sure I can get most NATO members to pay up their share of defense spending.
And then there's the tax cut. That's made a lot of people happy.
And tax receipts may be even higher because of it, it's happened before,
Not that I haven't pissed off a good share of folks, too, but that's part of my shtick.

He turns to look at the portrait of Andrew Jackson on the wall to his left.

He gets up and goes to stand before it. After a moment, he goes to sit on one of the chairs by the fireplace.

Not everyone has been a great President. I'm sure I won't be

the worst.
Do I like Putin?
He's a smooth operator. So I do like him.
But Melania's point is that, in the clutch, I blinked.
And she's right.
Being the President, I can be bossy with everyone under me.
I can say whatever I want and get away with it.
From here on out, and for the rest of my days, I'll have a security detail protecting me and I'll be able to say what I damn well please.
Not that that's ever stopped me.

He laughs.

So why did I hold back when the reporter asked the question in Helsinki?
Did I want to be nice to Putin?
Yes.
Does he have something on me?
No. He does not.
But my deepest fear is that the hacking was more extensive than it's been determined. And if that is so, then the argument that Putin swayed the election becomes stronger. Even if it can't be proven.
And he could say that he put me in the White House.

He shifts his weight on his seat.

My failing has been to not have been willing to publicly accept that possibility.
If Mueller ever came out with evidence of larger scale Russian machinations, then my election, and that of all Republican office holders, would be tarnished with the stain

of illegitimacy.
Cries would rise for me to surrender my post to Hillary.
Of course, I wouldn't do that because there would be no proof.
But I would go down in the history books as the interloper President.

He gets up and returns to his seat behind his desk.

I've liked it up here. It's been stressful, but it's been a lot of fun.
Deep down I've always felt that I got in on a fluke. Lost the popular vote by a good margin... which I've tried to blame on the undocumented.

He laughs.

I can come up with some good ones, can't I?
I'm feeling comfortable in this gig and wouldn't want to give it up. They'll have to kick me out.
I don't see how.

He pivots his chair to look out the window.

I can see why Putin wouldn't want to show his hand. He knows I'm insecure in my position... yep... he knows that... and he would like to work it to his advantage. He can just keep denying he knew anything and, in the meantime, do all he can to cover up the evidence so Mueller can't get to it. Whatever that might be.
But he could bring it out at any moment, if he so wished. He wouldn't dare show it to me, though... no, he's too smooth for that.

But who knows what he's capable of.

He sits back and runs his fingers through his hair.

Would everything I've done be invalidated?
Good question.
Everything I've done being erased. Wow. As if I'd never done anything.
The legal battles would be long and arduous, since every election could be contested.
The whole country would be thrust into a crisis.

He leans forward, elbows on knees, lacing his hands. He's tired.
He looks at his watch. It's 10 pm.
He gets up and stands before the window, looking out.

Putin had never interfered with an American election as he did in mine. Not that we know of… not on this scale.
But he saw the debates, the chaos and free for all, and he saw his opportunity. He must've said, 'I can fish in troubled waters'. And he threw in his hook.
I suspect it had my name on it.

He crosses his arms.

I could do what Melania is saying, do a complete turn around and embrace the Mueller probe.
But I'm scared.
Scared that they will find something…
And I can't get that monkey off my back.

A knock at the door.

**Donald** — Who is it?
**Melania** — It's me.
**Donald** — Come on in.

She steps in and goes to his side. She circles his waist with her arm and leans against his shoulder. They both stare out the window.

**Melania** — Pretty night.
**Donald** — Yes.

He puts his arm around her shoulders, presses her to him.

**Melania** — What have you been thinking?
**Donald** — Legitimacy.

She says nothing, and rubs gently the back of his neck.

**Donald** — I got in. Somehow. But something is missing.

They remain standing there for a moment.

**Melania** — Let's go to bed. It's late.

# 3

Donald is finishing addressing a huge rally, standing room only. A multitude of American flags are waving in the crowd. The noise dies down just so…

**Donald (into the mike)** — You know… I am here because of you… because you love me… and together… you and me… will Make America Great Again!

The crowd explodes in thunderous cries of USA! USA! Long live Trump! Long live the King! Streams of multicolored confetti shoot out into the arena below from contraptions set up high above and rousing music blares out from the loudspeakers.

He raises his arms and waves back, beaming with satisfaction, exulting in the crowd's adoration.
Then the room goes completely dark and the music stops.

Donald finds himself alone in a barely lit, rectangular room. There are no windows. He's seated in a chair at one end of the room.
He looks around warily but it's very dark. He's not sure of where he is or what he's doing there.
He feels something on his head, so he reaches up and removes it. He pulls it close to his eyes so he can examine it.

He smiles.

**Donald** — A crown… ah… finally…

Just then a tall, slender, and shadowy figure appears at the other end of the room. The Man is dressed in a black suit with a hood over his head. Donald is puzzled because he didn't see the Man enter.
The Man glances at him. With a wave of his hand the Man creates a chair for himself and sits facing Donald.
In the darkness, Donald cannot discern the Man's features. The Man calmly crosses his legs.

**Man** — You and me… working together… will make America great again…

The Man speaks with a deep, bass voice. Donald listens attentively.

**Man** — … so if your supporters had had a greater role in the conduct of the nation's affairs… the country would not have slipped from greatness?

Donald eyes the Man suspiciously.

**Man** — But how is that possible… that such a vital section of the nation allowed itself to be pushed aside… and by whom?
**Donald** — The immigrants, the undocumented, the illegals!

The Man shakes his head slowly.

**Man** — They have all that much political power?

Donald chuckles.

**Donald** — Who are you?

**Man** — You're running a scam in broad daylight, aren't you…?

Donald laughs.

**Donald** — (pressing) Who are you?
**Man** — … transferring blame to an important, productive and enterprising segment of the nation… to exonerate… excuse your base.
**Donald** — Watch your words, buddy… you'd get lynched if you said something like that at one of my rallies.
**Man** — I say exonerate and excuse because it's not the immigrants and minorities that's pushing your base down… and you know it… no… instead, it's been your base's affluent and politically powerful brothers and sisters… white also… who did not reach out to them and said… 'come, rise and walk with me'.
**Donald** — They've needed a leader…
**Man (skeptically)** — You?
**Donald** — Yes, me… to lead them out the wilderness and to the promised land. And if I have to blame some groups to stir them up, so be it.
**Man** — So you picked the easier target… rather than the class that has been deaf to their cries…

Donald, his anger smoldering, stares at the Man.

**Man** — … the class to which you belong.
**Donald (impatiently)** — Look… I'd love to chat but I'm a busy guy… I've got a country to run…
**Man** — So your base shares blame for not examining themselves… and waiting too long.
**Donald** — They've been waiting for me…

**Man** — Dear man... you're a choice of desperation... and not a good one.

**Donald** — I've had enough of this.

He tries to get up but can't.

**Donald** — What the hell?

There are no visible ties to bind him but he cannot get out of the chair. He struggles frantically but cannot free himself.

**Man** — The crowds at your rallies, do you promise them anything?
**Donald** — Why, yeah... sure, I tell them they can have... *we* can have... anything we want, if we stick together.
**Man** — I see the salesman in you.
**Donald** — As a matter of fact, I am. New York City salesman. Ever been to New York City? Ever heard of Trump Tower... I mean, where have you been? You've never heard of me?

The Man says nothing.

**Donald** — Look, buddy, I don't know what game you're playing but you can't just hold me down like this... I'm the president of the United States.
**Man** — I'm not holding you down.
**Donald (still trying in vain to free himself)** — You've no idea who you're messing with.
(bursting in anger)
Goddammit, are you deaf? I command you to let me the hell out of here!

The Man is unmoved.

Donald bows his head, gathering his strengths. Again, he thrusts forward trying to pull out of the chair but cannot.

**Donald** — Goddammit! Let me out!

The Man stares at Donald.
Frustrated, Donald tries another tack.

**Donald** — Say, friend… I didn't mean to get ornery… what's your name?

The Man rises slowly, starts to leave but then stops, still looking at Donald.

**Donald** — Who are you? (exasperated) What do you want from me?

The Man turns and vanishes.

**Donald** — Hey, you!

Donald wakes up with a startle, sitting up in bed, restless.
Melania is asleep next to him.
He then rises, puts on his robe and crosses to the window. He pulls up a chair and sits, looking out into the night.

# 4

Outside Moscow. Putin's dacha.

Putin's walking in the woods outside his home. Wearing a tee shirt and jeans, he is accompanied by his dog and a Woman dressed in a grey pant suit.
Putin stops, picks up a stick from the ground, rears back and calling to his dog, "Fetch boy, fetch!" hurls the stick a good distance off. The dog races after the stick.

**Putin** — How deep do you think the Mueller investigation will go?
**Woman** — He's stubborn. Diligent. He won't give up and won't be intimidated.
**Putin** — You think there's a chance they'll uncover the full extent?
**Woman** — There is.
**Putin** — We have to protect Trump, at whatever cost.
**Woman** — Of course.
**Putin** — The more divided Americans are, the better for us. Their focus as a nation will be less clear.
**Woman** — He's good at dividing.
**Putin** — Excellent.
**Woman** — There are some fringe white supremacy groups that could use financial support. We would make it look like it's coming from some obscure, wealthy southerner. All online, of course.
**Putin** — Let's stay away from that.
**Woman** — We can increase the conversation in support of Republican candidates… we don't want Republicans to lose the House or the Senate.

**Putin** — I wish they could come together to put an end to the probe. By whatever means. They know it's best for them. We're still looking at Mueller's background, see what we can use against him?
**Woman** — He's clean.
**Putin** — Keep looking.
**Woman** — Of course.

The dog returns with the stick in his mouth. Putin pats him on the head, takes the stick and hurls it off again. This time it lands in the water of a nearby lake. The dog races after it again.

**Putin** — The more Trump feels he won the election on his own, the less cooperative he's likely to be. Which brings me to the reason I called for you.
**Woman** — Please.
**Putin** — I need his tax returns.
**Woman** — Tax returns?
**Putin** — I'd like to take a look.
**Woman** — They're probably in a tightly guarded vault.
**Putin** — So?

The Woman smiles.

**Putin** — Melania would like a look, too.

The Woman laughs.

**Woman** — You'd like Trump to know we got them?
**Putin** — No… but I may want to release them to the public, through a third party, at the right time.
**Woman** — We'll get to it right away.

**Putin** — Thank you. That is all.

The Woman bows.

**Woman** — It's been a pleasure. Have a good day

The Woman turns and leaves.

Putin walks towards the lake where the dog is still struggling to retrieve the stick.

**Putin** — Washington! Come boy, come! Washington!

# 5

White House bedroom suite. Midday.

Melania is standing by the window.

**Melania** — It wasn't just once.
I've been willing to forgive… to see his affairs as indiscretions… but if it were me having the affair, it would be a far different matter. I would be called every name under the sun… and the howls would be unceasing.
The disparagement would come not only from men but from women, too. Holy women.

She reaches to the drape and pulls it more open.

How do we get rid of temptation?
Impossible.
So it takes intelligence, more so than morality, to see the greater good of maintaining a relationship.
But there have to be limits. Without limits then it's an open marriage and that is no marriage at all.
We need limits so we learn to hold our pain. Hold our pain so we can examine it. Examine it so we can process it.
If we set limits we have a chance. A chance to explore who we are… value what we find… and commit to fulfilling our potential.
And if we dare to act as catalysts for each other, then we can rightly claim that the partnership is fruitful.
Marriage as a partnership to help deliver ourselves onto the world.
Affairs and indiscretions will happen because we're flawed.

But without the willingness to examine the source of the affair, then the deceit is compounded and the relationship no longer has validity.

She turns, walks back into the room and sits at the table.

The theory is clear in my mind... the practice, though, is murky.

She holds her face in her hands for a moment, then, looking forward...

I am not happy. His affairs have been wounding... far deeper than I have acknowledged.

She sits back and folds her hands on her lap.

A while back he said he was going to publicly apologize for his behavior toward women... he even drew up a statement that I thought was quite good... but he hasn't done it.
He cannot find the strength in himself to go public with it.
His base forgives his behavior... or looks the other way... and I have too, but I can't anymore.
His behavior toward women was unacceptable and the nation deserves an apology. But there's no apology and instead it continues... the other day he called a lady and former aide, a dog. What is that? Where does that come from?
He has no respect for the office he holds.
No concern for the role model he needs to be.

She rises and walks off a few paces.

I've talked myself into thinking I can have an impact on him but it's amounted to nothing. And yet I try... because I have a responsibility to the nation... to this country that took me in as an immigrant. I have a responsibility to act within my powers... to persuade him to come to his senses.

Tears have come to her eyes. She dabs them dry.

I've loved him... but I don't think he loves me... not anymore... if he did he would pay more attention... though sometimes he has... but he could be doing so much more.

She crosses to sit on the edge of the bed, arms on her knees.

Soon enough his base will tire of him... soon enough they'll see through him... they'll see that to deliver what they truly need he has to have the consent of the entire nation... because it's going to take a long term investment to empower them... and he doesn't know how to do that.
He knows how to whip up a rage against immigrants... but doesn't know how to constructively channel those energies. He can build hotels... but he doesn't know how to nurture people.
He knows how to use them... and yet... I love him.

She shakes her head slowly.

One day, though... I may choose not to be at his side.

# 6

Washington DC. Park. Evening.

A man in a suit (1st) sits at a bench. He checks his cell phone. A moment later, a second man (2nd), also in a suit, approaches and sits next to the first one. They both turn off their cell phones and lay them side to side between them.

**1st** — Pleasant evening.
**2nd** — Indeed.
**1st** — The investigation keeps going deeper.
**2nd** — Like it or not.
**1st** — They may yet stumble into something big.
**2nd** — Any day now.
**1st** — The democrats are salivating.
**2nd** — Drooling.
**1st** — Think Cohen will make a dent?
**2nd** — I think we've seen all he's got… but he may yet have an ace up his sleeve.
**1st** — Something's about to break.
**2nd** — How you think T will react?
**1st** — He'll go bonkers.

They look at each other.

**1st** — We'll have to ease him out. In the interest of the nation.
**2nd** — Like it or not.
**1st** — Call in a forensic team… certify him unfit for office.
**2nd** — There's a way to do it.
**1st** — I heard about it.

**2ⁿᵈ** — Pence should slide right in.
**1ˢᵗ** — We can work with him.
**2ⁿᵈ** — For a while.
**1ˢᵗ** — Mitch is whom I'd like to see as Prez.

They both chuckle.

**1ˢᵗ** — Hard to drain the swamp, ain't it?
**2ⁿᵈ** — Damn hard.

Two joggers pass by.

**1ˢᵗ** — You still jog?
**2ⁿᵈ** — Three times a week.
**1ˢᵗ** — I need to get back to it.
**2ⁿᵈ** — Good for your brain.
**1ˢᵗ** — What about Manafort?
**2ⁿᵈ** — Hard fall from grace.
**1ˢᵗ** — What a lousy vetting job, getting him for campaign manager.
**2ⁿᵈ** — You're not kidding. Where was the party?
**1ˢᵗ** — La La land.
**2ⁿᵈ** — Bet you he didn't jog.
**1ˢᵗ** — Manafort?
**2ⁿᵈ** (**smiling**) — Didn't get enough oxygen up there.

A squirrel scampers across.

**1ˢᵗ** — Think he'll get a pardon?
**2ⁿᵈ** — He just might.
**1ˢᵗ** — If he doesn't, it's going to be some years in uniform.
**2ⁿᵈ** — What a come down.
**1ˢᵗ** — I'm sure he saw himself slipping…

**2ⁿᵈ** — And he couldn't stop.
**1ˢᵗ** — Tragic character... when you can't stop yourself.
**2ⁿᵈ** — Playing out as we speak.
**1ˢᵗ** — Was it John Acton who said 'power tends to corrupt...' or was it Clausewitz?
**2ⁿᵈ** — John Acton. 'Absolute power corrupts absolutely'.
**1ˢᵗ** — Easy to forget... when you're counting the money.
**2ⁿᵈ** — Let's make sure it doesn't happen to us.
**1ˢᵗ** — Yep.
**2ⁿᵈ** — Will you call me aside if you see me slipping... if I ever do?
**1ˢᵗ** — I promise.
**2ⁿᵈ** — I'll do the same for you.
**1ˢᵗ** — Thanks.

He pauses.

I was about to say it won't ever happen to me...
but that's a bad sign right there.

They laugh.

**2ⁿᵈ** — Yep.
**1ˢᵗ** — Keep it real.
**2ⁿᵈ** — Amen.

# 7

White House. Dining room. Evening.

Donald and Melania having dinner. They sit next to each other. No one else is in the room.

**Melania** — You have good ideas.
**Donald** — What? Did I hear you correctly?

She smiles.

**Melania** — You do. I have been following the trade issue. China has been cheating us. Not only stealing our technology through forced transfers but also by heavily subsidizing industries that dump their cheap products onto our markets. You have brought attention to that. That's good.
**Donald** — Thank you, Melania. Thank you very much.
**Melania** — But the urgent need is to unite the nation… to help us reach our collective, higher self… which is where our greater riches lie.

He nods thoughtfully, then raises his glass of cider for a toast.

**Donald** — Here's to my winning the trade war.
**Melania** (**not raising her glass**) — Not in favor.
**Donald** (**smiling**) — Can't you just indulge your husband?
**Melania** — I have my political views.

He drinks.

**Melania** — You're also combative and feisty, and that has

mobilized something deep in the American psyche.
**Donald** — Thank you.
**Melania** — The nation was due for a good, internal fight, and we're having it now. I think that's why so many people voted for you.
**Donald** — That's two compliments in one evening. I'm marking this day in my calendar.

She smiles.

**Melania** — People identified with you because you represent something raw. A will to make money, to push ahead, even if it means you rough up some folks along the way.
**Donald** — That I've done.
**Melania** — Even your lack of refinement has an appeal.
**Donald (taken aback)** — I'm not refined?
**Melania** — Of course not. But that's part of your charm.
**Donald (a dash of regret)** — I always wanted to be refined.
**Melania** — Let it be. It's not in you. Obama, on the other hand, is refined.
**Donald (irritated)** — What?
**Melania** — He is. Look at his manner, his intellect, his gift for nuance and oratory.
**Donald (stubbornly)** — I am smart in my own way.
**Melania** — Of course you are. And it's okay not to be on the same level as Obama.
**Donald** — You're really coming after me, aren't you?
**Melania** — Not at all. I love you. You're just different.
**Donald** — Different?
**Melania** — Yes.

They pause, look at each other.

**Melania** — Go ahead, say it.
**Donald** — Say what?
**Melania** — That you're different.
**Donald** — I'm not going to say it.
**Melania** — It'll be good for you.
**Donald** — I'm not saying it.
**Melania** — Please.

He rubs his face, then smiles devilishly.

**Donald** — I am different.
**Melania** — Good.
A lot of people love you just as you are. Raw. Unrefined. And it's okay.
Being who you are, touches their hearts. Americans elected Obama twice, because they wanted to be like the man.
**Donald** — White people wanted to be like him?
**Melania** — He couldn't have got elected without white people.
**Donald** — True.
**Melania** — White people with prejudices, looked at Obama and said,
'now, that's a fellow I want to be like, even if he's dark.'
And the thought astonished them because they saw how the power of the mind overcame the racial barrier. And why had they not done it before? Why had they overlooked the possibilities of education? Like during Reconstruction after the Civil War?
**Donald** — Blacks wanted too much… too soon…
**Melania** — What's too soon about wanting the white man's boot off your throat?

**Donald** — Change takes time…

**Melania** — Social courage is what went missing.
But to my point… it's hard to be like Obama. Certainly not in just 8 years. It's going to take a lot longer and some heavy spending on education.
It didn't help that Republicans in both houses, filled with envy, decided to obstruct everything the man wanted to do during his term, as if they had said, 'how dare the upstart address our structural problems'.

**Donald** — They did obstruct him, I admit.

**Melania** — Republicans were dead set against spending because it would raise the deficit and how immoral it would be to burden our children with debt. Spending which, by the way, would have benefited your base also. Then you come along, cut taxes, the deficit goes through the roof and everyone is cheering, right?

He smiles with satisfaction.

**Donald** — Very soon, our coffers will be brimming.

**Melania** — It could go the other way.

**Donald** — It won't.

**Melania** — Let's hope.
The nation was not ready for more Obama, and Hillary came close to that.

**Donald** — Wait a second… Hillary is more refined than I am?

**Melania** — Yes.

He slaps the table in exasperation.

**Donald** — No she's not!

**Melania** — In the eyes of the nation, electing a woman was a further refinement in our collective thinking. But it was too much. The psyche of the white American voter had found it difficult, having been governed for 8 years by a refined African American, the mere sight of whom was a reminder that white supremacy is an absurdity, to have him then be followed by a woman. No. Unacceptable. The psyche of the average white American voter needed time to readjust... and in the absence of visionary candidates... chose to regress.

**Donald** — Regress?

**Melania** — Yes.

**Donald** — So I'm a regression?

**Melania** — A symbol of it.

**Donald** — That's insulting.

**Melania** — Sadly it came with a price... the targeting of minorities, the sanctioning of crude behavior against women, the further breakdown in the national dialogue.

**Donald** — You're wrong, Melania... very wrong... yes, we needed a good fight... but we did because we were growing weak... and seeing that – which was my great insight — I reached down into our collective unconscious and stirred up the spirit of the frontier... I alone stirred up the feistiness, the greed and the combativeness that had made us great.

The look at each other for a moment.

**Melania** — But the world has changed, my dear... these are not the days of the frontier and that is not lost on white Americans. They know they have to change also.
They know that in a few decades' time, they will be a minority in this country.

**Donald** — We cannot have that.

She smiles.

**Melania** — It's beyond you. You know that.
White Americans know, that for the nation to remain an engine of growth and a dominant world economy, we need the strong back of foreigners, be they Mexicans, Latin Americans, Arabs, Africans or Asians.
White American women are simply not willing to devote their lives to popping out enough white children to take their places, and they're not because they've discovered the pleasures and challenges of the mind.

He put his elbows on the table, joining his hands. Staring off, he nods slightly.

**Donald** — So I'm a transitional figure... so to speak.
**Melania** — That's a good way to put it.
White America was essential to bringing the country to where it is now... and that achievement is its glory — leaving out the century of slavery and the century of Jim Crow — but they know that to continue to move forward, we need the world.
Change is at our core.
And part of the genius of the American mind has been to recognize the virtue of being inclusive.

He rises and walks off a few paces.

**Melania** — China's on our heels... and now, more than ever, we need openness... the belief in the nation's transformative powers... the powers that nurture us... and which take the immigrant and makes them our brothers and sisters.

He turns around to face Melania who's still seated at the

table.

**Donald** — Let's see how China survives the tariffs.
**Melania** — They stole technology from us but their talents knew how to take it and add value to it. And if they ever need the strong backs of other nations, they will invite them in. They know what isolation is. They paid dearly for it in the past.-

He nods thoughtfully.

**Donald** — You think I'll get reelected?
**Melania** — Doubt it.
**Donald** — How come?
**Melania** — We're getting tired of your antics and want to get back to the business of nation building.
**Donald** — If I build the wall I'll have a better chance.

Melania stares at him.

**Donald** — Mind you, I know we don't need a wall… but I'll give them a wall anyway… a huge and expensive one… the more the better… so that my people can flock over and admire it, touch it, kiss it, climb on it, take selfies with it in the background. And Mexicans will build the wall… our Mexicans… because we need their labor… and at night their cousins and friends will find a way to climb up on top of it and drop down onto our soil. And we'll catch them and send them back… only so they climb back up once more and do it all over again… because so long as our economy is stronger than theirs, the flow will not cease.
I know that. My people know that, too.
**Melania** — But still you will build it…

**Donald (smugly)** — I keep my promises.
**Melania** — Billions of dollars that could go to training programs... for education...
**Donald** — And they will reelect me.
**Melania** — Why not give them the money instead?
**Donald** — They're all good people... but they've been neglected for too long.
**Melania** — Neglected you say... by whom may I ask?
**Donald** — Why, by the political class...
**Melania** — ... and the affluent... both of whom happen to be mostly white...
so is it fair to point the finger at immigrants and minorities?

He gives her a long look.

**Donald** — Whoever said life was fair?
**Melania** — Understood. So maybe you should say that at your rallies, too.

He laughs.

**Donald** — You know... the democrats have an up and coming socialist wing... you might be interested in joining.

She rises.

**Melania** — Let's go for a walk.

They exit and a moment later they're walking in the White House garden, side by side.

**Donald** — How do you think Helsinki's playing in the White American psyche?

**Melania** — Remember Charlottesville?
**Donald** — August 12$^{th}$, 2017, how could I forget?
**Melania** — You equivocated then also.
**Donald** — Equivocated?
**Melania** — Both sides were at fault, you said then. Couldn't commit. Same as in Helsinki.
**Donald** — So?
**Melania** — So the White American psyche is wondering… what's with the waffling?

He stops and so does she.

**Donald** — You have said that you believe me when I say I didn't collude…
**Melania** — I stand by that.
**Donald** — But do you think… even if it cannot be proven… that Russia's interference in the election threw it my way?
**Melania** — I do.

He grimaces as he studies her expression… then takes a step back.

**Donald** — I know you're unhappy. So why are you sticking around?
**Melania** — Because I still think that you can be a good president.
**Donald** — Melania… I don't think it's in me to be a cheerleader for Mueller and his probe…
I don't think it's in me to be a builder of dialogue between Right and Left…
I appreciate your good intentions but that's not going to happen.

I'd rather lose the next election than compromise on what I believe.
And I don't think I'm committing political suicide.
I think we will win and keep control of both houses… and victory will mean more deregulation and more defense spending, more tax cuts and less welfare, less foreign aid and more restrictive immigration… and that's what I want to do… and if I go out after one term, so be it… but I am not going out… so I'll have another term to choose even more supreme court justices, so my legacy will be enduring.
I happen to like a bit of chaos in my life… and that's who I am.
And I happen to think that most Americans want what I want… chaos included.
And if down the line, reality tells us that we have to change course, then we'll do so, but for now we're doing just fine… breaking down boundaries… pushing the limits.

He pauses.

Am I being too blunt?
**Melania** — Not at all. It's best to know where I stand.
**Donald** — This is not an act that I'm putting on, Melania… this is who I am… and the great white American psyche seems to like me. Regression or not. Refinement or not.

She looks at the ground for a moment.

**Donald** — As far as inequality is concerned, I'm all for it. Some people have more drive than others and more brains than others and more imagination than others… and those people need plenty of rewards so they can keep creating wealth for everybody else… not that we don't need the less

gifted too, sure we do, and the more educated they are the more they'll learn to tame their resentments... the more they'll learn to put up with their unsolved grievances...
But most Americans want to be rich... like me... not do-gooders... even if it means stepping on others as they climb. The really smart figure it out... they always have... they get on with it and don't complain...
so it has been for ever and ever... and so it will be... for ever and ever.

She looks him in the eye.

**Donald** — The trade war is just the beginning... and I will make alliances with the wealthy and creative all over the world... and my people will love me for that... because deep in their hearts and minds... that's how they see themselves.
**Melania** — Even if the majority will never get there.
**Donald** — You die trying.
**Melania** — I suppose, then, that you have no intention of making a public apology to American women, like you once said you would?
**Donald** — I've gone back and forth on that... but I don't think so.
**Melania** — Why not?
**Donald** — Because powerful men have privileges...
**Melania** — The privilege to harass...?
**Donald** — If you let me get away with it.
And if women don't like it then go ahead and bitch, and march and complain and unite and form a political party if you want... and let's fight it out.
I have no idea of where that will end... maybe it will end in some kind of new sexual equality...
But you have to fight for it...

And to be frank… why shouldn't you win that fight?
You're a greater number than men in this country.

He pauses.

But something holds you back.
Why did Hillary lose?
It wasn't Russian interference… it was because women let themselves down. But nobody's talking about that. I do not hear women criticizing themselves, lamenting that they didn't seize the opportunity.
**Melania** — Excuse me, I was the one who made that point about women.
**Donald** — You did. And a good one it was, too.
Hillary wasn't perfect, we all know that, but she was a seasoned politician… a woman who had been through some tough fights in her life…
And her own kind just blew her off.
Instead of saying, 'okay, Hillary has some flaws, but she's a woman's woman for crying out loud, so let's go with her!', instead of doing that, you waffled… and I got in.

He smiles with satisfaction.

**Donald** — So I owe much to waffling.
**Melania** — It's coming back to haunt you.

He walks off a few paces, then turns around to face her again.

**Donald** — What happened to your women's party, a while back you talked about getting one going?
**Melania** — I did talk about it… and you asked me not to do

it.
**Donald** — Well… you need to do what you think is right.
**Melania** — Yes.

She walks over to the window, crosses her arms as she looks out, pensively.

**Donald** — Go for it. See if women can really unite… not just talk about it and complain about what men do and don't do.

She pulls open the drapes a little more. She doesn't look at him as she speaks.

**Melania** — Women have never stopped fighting. Nature put the fight in us… not only to struggle to be all we can be but also to take pause at some point during our lifetime… to create human beings and to nurture them… and it is a noble fight indeed… so no, we're no stranger to the good fight.
We raise and nurture you and all men alike… only to see you then turn around and devalue us… do violence to us, as if you were ashamed of your origins. Man's story, is the story of denying us opportunity… denying us access to education, access to the vote, denying us equal pay, denying us control over our bodies… we've had to fight for every single one of those gains… and it has gone on and on and to this day… so don't you dare sing the praises of inequality when you have known nothing but privilege… and know nothing about the treasures hidden in those who have been deemed less gifted. It's painful to see you stand there and carry on with your drivel …
For it speaks loudly of your disconnect with history…

And when you justify your crude behavior toward women…
And then have the audacity to ask us to fight some more…
speaking as if you were exempt from examining yourself and finding fault with your own behavior.

She turns to look at him.

There is a profound rift in the nation…
And you intend to address it by telling us that putting more money in our pockets is the solution.

She holds her face in her hands and then slowly brushes back her hair.
He walks over to stand by her side.

**Donald** — I didn't mean to offend you.
**Melania** — You did.
You paint yourself as the great fighter… but tell me… was that you fighting Putin in Helsinki?
**Donald** — Putin is part of the elite of this world… like it or not. He's sitting on top of a lot of gas and oil and a lot of nuclear weapons… and like him or not… he's managed to convince a lot of Russians to cheer him on. And he has growing fans in other nations as well. That's reality.
**Melania** — So you give him a pass?
**Donald** — He's got nothing on me. Even if he's lying and did know of the interference in our election… or directed it… I got in on my own… and I couldn't have done it without American women.

She nods slowly.

**Donald** — If you ever get it together on the idea of the

Women's party... that should be up there on the agenda to discuss.

**Melania** — Feeling pretty confident, aren't you?

**Donald** — Why shouldn't I? GDP went over 4 percent, bull market is going strong... NATO members are paying up on defense... I'm renegotiating NAFTA... unemployment is low... and people have more money in their pockets. America is finding itself again.

He goes to her, gives her a kiss on the forehead.

**Donald** — I'll be at the office for a while.

And he exits.

# 8

Oval Office. White House. Night.

He goes in and sits at his desk. He pushes back on the chair and puts his feet up.

**Donald** — Annoying as it is sometimes, it's useful to hear that liberal point of view. Not that she doesn't have some good ideas.
What I said about American women giving me a free pass, at least the ones in my base,
that's true.
And I got in. Love them.
How did Melania put it? Something about women feeling suppressed for so long that they could not bring themselves to choose one of their own.
Interesting how that view doesn't get any press... wonder why?
Maybe their less suppressed sisters just being nice and tolerant.

He laughs.

Madeline Albright came up with that line that women who didn't vote for Hillary deserved a place in hell. Got you, babe.
The women in my base were being pragmatic... that's what it was... they knew that what I brought to the table was far more important than those peccadilloes...

He pauses, then glances over his shoulder at the portrait of

Andrew Jackson.

What say you, Stonewall?

He gets up and goes to stand in front of the portrait.
Speaking to Jackson…

You held back the British in New Orleans, and I will hold back immigration.
Stonewall they nicknamed you,
and surely they'll come up with something for me,
something to immortalize me…
Because the wall goes, brother, I promise you that.

Jackson winks back at him.

# 9

Park in Washington DC. Early evening. A middle aged man and a woman, walking side by side approach an empty bench. They both wear business suits. They sit, both take out their phones, turn them off and place them between them.

**Man** — You can smell blood, can't you?
**Woman** — There's that scent.
**Man** — If we win both houses we'll have a chance to impeach him…
**Woman** — Manafort, Cohen, Gates… the dominoes are falling.
**Man** — Man going down and can't stop himself. How many times have we seen it?
**Woman** — He made his choices… now he's got to live with them.
**Man** — We've got to win in November, though.
**Woman** — Have to pull all the stops.
You think he colluded?
**Man** — I didn't think so, but since Helsinki I've changed my mind.

A man with a child in a stroller go by.

**Man** — Russians want him in… so there's going to be a massive effort to support him.
**Woman** — What would you do?
**Man** — My take… go straight to the people sitting on the fence, tell them 'this is who your leader is. A vote against Trump is a vote against Russia's interference, a vote against Trump is a vote for a sovereign America.'

**Woman** — You'd concede the base…?

**Man** — Pretty much. Run the video clip of Helsinki… 'if he can't stand up to Putin, will he stand up for you?' Brand him an appeaser.

**Woman** — 'Hey John Voter, wake up, buddy! Trump's doing a number on you. He's given you a platform to rant and rave but who's listening? You're going nowhere with the hooting and hollering. He's cranking you up but where are you headed?

**Man** — Go check out the wall.

**Woman** — Right.

**Man** — Where are the programs to get you up to speed on the global economy? Where is the education you need?

**Woman** — Basic stuff.

They look at each other.

**Man** — The Street loves him.

**Woman** — Sure, they got their tax cut and deregulations.

**Man** — The economy is going strong… can't take that away from him.
You and I are worked up about him but people like to hear that jingle in their pocket… and may be willing to look the other way.

**Woman** — True.

A young couple in love saunters by.

The Man and the Woman glance at each other and smile.

**Man** — How'd we get here?

**Woman** — The debates. Not a single one of them stood up to Trump. Not a single one took him to task.

**Man** — Clinton should've made mincemeat out of him but she didn't. And that was it.
**Woman** — Comey put the last shovel full of dirt on her.
**Man** — Unbelievable.

Pause.

**Man (singing)** — What a difference a day makes… twenty four little hours…
**Woman** — It's sad.
**Man** — Well… it's payback time… there's a lot of angry women running for office.
**Woman** — As they should.

An elderly, frail looking woman walks past with the aid of a cane. She limps a little.

The man and the woman look at her.

# 10

Donald walks into a large room in the Kremlin. In the center, there are two seats facing a small table with two bottles of water. In one of the chairs sits Putin who now rises to greet the advancing Donald. The two men shake hands. Putin signals for Donald to take a seat.
No translators are present.

**Donald** — Glad you could make it.
**Putin** — For you, anytime.
**Donald** — Thanks.
**Putin** — What can I do for you?
**Donald** — I'll get straight to the point.
**Putin** — Please.
**Donald** — You interfered with our elections in 2016.
**Putin** — I did.

Donald is surprised.

**Donald** — You have been denying it all this time…
**Putin** — We were in public. In private, it's a different matter. That's the beauty of meeting alone.

Putin smiles.

**Donald** — You can't do that.
**Putin** — I did it.
**Donald** — Why?
**Putin** — It was wide open. Low lying fruit, as you Americans say. How could I resist? I'm an old KGB hand. You're not exactly new to intrigue but, next to me, you're a

newbie.

Donald is disconcerted.

**Putin** — Look at it this way, real wars are bloody and painful. We both have a long history of it. In WWII alone, Mother Russia lost 20 million people. Hard to imagine, isn't it? Your country has never suffered a loss of that magnitude. Of course, we would do it again if we needed to, but cyberwarfare is so much cleaner.
And more effective.
**Donald** — What are you after?

Putin smiles warmly.

**Donald (pressing)** — What are you after?
**Putin** — Don't you know?
**Donald** — I am asking.
**Putin** — The American mind.

Donald stares at Putin.

**Donald (emphatically)** — You can't have it!

Putin nods thoughtfully.

**Putin** — My cyber warriors will see to it… and it can't be stopped.
**Donald** — Can't be stopped?
**Putin** — Historical forces beyond my control, and yours, have been set in motion. Believe me, we're mere pawns
**Donald** — Pawns?
**Putin** — There's two sides to your famous America, one

side that wants education and fairness of opportunity... so the motivated and capable can climb up the ladder... and another side, sitting on top, that loves to knock down the ladder... so no one but the favorites will follow.
So you fluctuate between being a meritocracy... very honorable, of course... and a nepotocracy.

**Donald** — Nepotocracy?

**Putin** — Ring a bell?

**Donald** — What?

**Putin** — That's the side you and I are with.

Donald rises abruptly.

**Donald** — I'm not listening to this. I'm leaving.

He turns and stalks to the door. But the door is locked and he can't open it.

**Donald** — Let me out!

He slams his fist on the door but there's no response.

Putin, unconcerned with Donald's pleas but affecting a sympathetic air, rises and takes a few steps toward him.

**Putin** — Please listen, this is the most important part. The two sides have tried to dialogue... and sometimes they've succeeded... and when they have, the American mind has been brilliant... like in battling the Depression... and in World War II... and the Marshall plan afterwards... but at other times you've been a disaster... like in dealing with racism.

Donald advances toward Putin with determined step and the two men come face to face.

**Donald** — We defeated you in the Cold War! Our economy left you behind!
**Putin (gently)** — Yes, you did. You crushed us. You were the victor. I accept it.
**Donald** — Thank you.
**Putin** — My dear and beautiful Soviet Union… broken up into pieces.
It was very sad and painful to see it happen. And the whole world stood witness.

Putin turns around and returns to his seat. He resumes speaking, now and then glancing up at Donald who remains standing near him.

**Putin** — That was the American mind at work…
The American mind that does science… and art… and the humanities… the mind that is intoxicated with the pursuit of riches… any and all types of riches… the mind that takes on any challenge… the cradle of Intel and IBM and Boeing and Northrop… and the miracles in food production and medicine… and MIT and Cal Tech and JPL… and Apple, Google, and Microsoft, Amazon, Tesla and Hollywood…
The insatiable American mind that wants to dominate and transform the world… devour us all… to impose your culture…

Putin looks Donald in the eye.

**Putin** — The insatiable mind that seduces talent from everywhere… from Russia too… my dear Russia…

Immigrants flocking to your country lured by your way of life...
Believe me, we lament their leaving...
And most of all, lament that they don't return.
Your gains my dear sir... and our losses.

Donald narrows his eyes, warily.

**Putin** — Who knows what would've happened if Sergey hadn't left...
**Donald** — Sergey?
**Putin** — Brin. The cofounder of Google. Born right here in my Moscow.
**Donald** — He got out. He went to Stanford.
**Putin (smiling slyly)** — It will take time, of course... but we will do it...
**Donald** — Do what?
**Putin** — ... with great stealth...
**Donald** — What?
**Putin** — ... my cyber warriors... will work to steadily erode your values... but it's for the good of the world, you must understand... so that we create a level playing field... because you're too much out in front... and the cyber warriors will do so by targeting your culture... accentuating your differences... minimizing your similarities... so your dialogue will be impoverished ... degraded... and finally stopped.

Putin pauses

**Donald** — Stop our dialogue?
**Putin** — The pearl that lies at the center of it all... the light that when shining shows you the way.

When it goes out... for it will... I will rejoice as I never have. Or rather, the mere pawn that I am will rejoice.
**Donald** — I won't let you.
**Putin** — In the chaos that will follow... in the darkness... your people will clamor for autocracy... a wonderful system... vastly underrated... a system where the majority rules... and minorities learn to live with it... suck it up... as you're fond of saying.
**Donald (to himself, considering it)** — A world where the autocrat is the light...
**Putin** — Yes! Brilliant! Oh dear man, you're so much like me... that's why I like you so... that's why we're so fond of each other.
Every time you cry out 'Fake News!' my heart leaps with joy.
**Donald** — It does?
**Putin** — Yes! Believe me, I'm rooting for you to succeed, you have my full backing.

Donald steps back, shaking his head, distrustful.

**Donald** — No... no... there's something wrong here... you're tricking me...
**Putin** — Donald... please... I am eager to learn from you... I tape all your rallies...
**Donald** — You tape my rallies?
**Putin** — Yes. So I can study them... and learn to work a crowd... learn to please it... to excite it... for you are the master... the one and only... oh, how I wish I had your gifts!
**Donald (moved)** — I am very good.
**Putin** — An artist.
**Donald** — Thank you. Did you know that I have a star in Hollywood's Walk of Fame?
**Putin** — Of course I know. They should add a statue.

Donald frowns, suspicion growing again.

**Putin** — I owe you more than you owe me.
**Donald** — I owe *you*?
**Putin** — It's nothing… nothing compared to what you give us… and are giving us… by your example… every day… how you rose from nothing…
**Donald** — Nothing?
**Putin** — I mean, from being a distinguished hotelier and shrewd judge of character… Manafort and Gates aside… to beating, smashing the Clinton machine.
**Doanld** — Thank you.
**Putin** — You're most welcome. And I'm so sorry… we tried to get you the popular vote, we really did… but it was not possible. I know you wanted it badly. I'm so sorry.

Donald explodes with anger.

**Donald** — What? How dare you? You did not win me the election! American women did!

**Putin** — There's no need to get upset. We will do much better next time, I assure you. We're already working on it, improving our techniques.
**Donald (loudly)** — You will not interfere with our elections, do you hear me?
**Putin (rising, stepping up to Donald)** — Please lower your voice. For your own good, Donald. You're overweight and out of shape… and I wouldn't want you to have a heart attack. I'm serious. You're too valuable an asset.

**Donald** — Asset?

Fuming, trying to control his rage, Donald paces off for a stretch, then turns to face Putin again.

**Donald** — Are we being recorded?
**Putin** — I record all my conversations.

Donald is incredulous.

**Putin** — For history's sake, believe me, because we're on the right side of history, you and I, don't you ever doubt it. Would you like a glass of cider? A bit of caviar?
**Donald** — No!
**Putin** — Calm down, it will be all right.

Donald stares angrily at Putin.

**Putin** — We need to be composed when we step out for the press conference.
**Donald (panicking)** — Press conference?

White House. Bedroom.

Abruptly, Donald sits up in his bed, confused and agitated.

**Donald (crying out)** — Helsinki! Helsinki!

Melania is by his side, holding him.

**Melania** — You're here, you're not in Helsinki! Dee, you're here with me, in our bedroom!

He gives a shudder and turns to face her.

**Donald** — What happened?
**Melania** — It must've been a bad dream.
**Donald** — A dream?
**Melania** — You've been shouting Helsinki! Helsinki!
**Donald** — A dream… yes… thank god… but it was so real.
**Melania** — What happened?
**Donald** — What else did I say?
**Melania** — Just that.

He falls back down on the bed, immensely relieved, the face sweaty with perspiration.

**Donald** — I didn't say anything else?
**Melania** — No… just Helsinki.

She gets up, put her robe on and crosses to sit at his side. She holds his face in her hands and kisses him.

**Melania** — I'm so sorry. Why don't you talk about it?
**Donald** — I can't remember anything… did you hear anything else?
**Melania** — No. Just Helsinki.

He sighs, shakes his head, the expression still strained. He looks at her and takes her hands in his and kisses them.

**Donald** — Thank you. Wow. I felt so alone.
**Melania** — Talk about what you remember… maybe the whole dream will come back.
**Donald** — I can't remember anything. What time is it?
**Melania** — Five am.
**Donald** — Might as well get up, then.

He does and walks to the table adjacent where he sits, his worries weighing on him.

**Melania** — What a coincidence…
**Donald** — What?
**Melania** — Helsinki is 7 hours ahead… the dream happened about the same time you held that news conference on July 16th.

Donald looks at her, baffled.

# 11

White House. Evening. South Lawn. Three weeks later.

Donald and Melania are walking alongside.

**Melania** — What was the point of insulting Lebron James, the basketball player?
**Donald** — It got away from me.
**Melania** — The man had just helped fund a school for underprivileged children…
**Donald** — Please, stop.
**Melania** — It is so unbecoming of a President.

They walk in silence.

**Melania** — And then you keep having those rallies…
**Donald** — We need to win in November. Both houses. I love my rallies… stirring up their fury… love it… and with every rally I validate them…
**Melania** — Validate them?
**Donald** — Sure… that they've been treated unfairly, like I have, Clinton's 'deplorables,' how could you forget? And by extension the witch hunt…
**Melania** — By extension?

She stops. He does, too.

**Melania** — Are you linking Hillary and Mueller?
**Donald** — Put her in jail! they chant, again and again.
**Melania** — Russian talk about their having damaging emails on Hillary started the investigation… but Mueller's

probe is not about Hillary's campaign, it's about yours…
and if you link them to stir up your base, then you're guilty
of manipulating their admiration for you and should be
ashamed of yourself.
Hillary is one thing, the probe quite another… which your
own attorney general recused himself from overseeing… and
you can't stop badgering him for… which smells of a clear
intent to cover up.

He looks at her, then lowers his head as he pinches the base
of his nose.

**Donald (calmly but with an edge to his voice)** — It's a
witch hunt… a rigged witch hunt… and neither I nor anyone
working on my instructions obstructed justice. That's all you
need to know.
**Melania** — No, it's not. And you're not brushing me off.

They stand glaring at each other.

**Donald** — So I'm guilty?
**Melania** — You're acting like it.
**Donald (irritated)** — Why don't you just go back to New
York and leave me alone?
**Melania** — I'm staying right here.
I am your wife and there's something wrong with you.
I'm not about to abandon ship.

He shakes his head slowly.

**Melania** — And now you've started to have those dreams.
**Donald** — I've only had three or four…
**Melania** — How about seven or eight?

**Donald** — They're not coming back. I know that.
**Melania** — You have no control over them.
**Donald** — Yes, I do.
**Melania** — What are the dreams about?
**Donald** — I can't remember anything.
**Melania** — Then how the heck can you have control over them?
**Donald** — I just do.
**Melania** — Nonsense.
**Donald (angrily)** — You are not inside my mind, Melania! I do not remember my dreams, okay?
I do not.
**Melania** — Then you can't have control over them.
**Donald** — Yes, I can.
**Melania** — How?
**Donald** — Because after every rally, after I vent my frustrations, I go for at least two or three nights without any nightmares.
**Melania** — So you'll need to keep having rally after rally… whipping your base into a rage… so you can sleep better at night… is that it?
**Donald** — I think they'll fade.
**Melania** — You'll beat down your dreams with the help of your adoring crowds.
**Donald** — Something like that.

They are quiet for a moment.

**Melania** — It is madness… pure madness.
**Donald** — You want me to see a psychiatrist, is that it?
**Melania** — Why not? You have nothing to lose. You seem unable to reflect on what's happening even as it's staring you in the face, even as you're heading for a head on collision…

so maybe... maybe... speaking to someone like that might help you save your Presidency.

He just looks at her.

**Melania (gently)** — Dee... the party will not do it for you. They're probably already plotting against you.
**Donald** — I don't doubt it... but they won't get away with it.

She closes in and puts her hands on his shoulders.

**Melania** — There's still time... to find your higher self... I know it's in you... reach for it... please... it's there. Beneath the hooting and hollering of your adoring crowds... lies a desire for clarity... a yearning for connection with themselves and their fellow human beings... you can lead them there... but you can't do it if you haven't found that place in yourself.
Do you understand what I'm saying?

He nods uncertainly.

**Melania** — Doing that... is more important than your presidency.
**Donald (softly, incredulously)** — What?
**Melania** — You owe your base complete honesty... they brought you this far... it's been an incredible ride... you never imagined it would be this rich... they made you president... but dark clouds have gathered over you and you have to answer with honesty... you owe them that... and what will be will be. They have been disappointed by others that came before you... don't join in with those... you have

a unique chance to do the right thing... and that would be priceless. And no matter what... I'll stand by you.
Look at me, do you believe me?
**Donald** — I don't know... I've cheated on you so many times... disrespected you...
**Melania** — And still I love you... and believe in you.

She takes his hands in hers and kisses them as she looks up at him.

**Melania** — Dee... I'm here because of you... I'm not a hostage to this glamour.
**Donald** — Melania... I appreciate what you're telling me... but it's going to be okay... I'm making money for my people... that's what really counts...
**Melania** — No!

She pulls away brusquely and stalks off a few paces before she pivots to face him again.

**Melania** — You're leading a nation, not a company!
We need more than money... we need a sense that we care for each other...
A sense that we share a truth! That we're a community!
Because it's not every man for himself... it can't be...
We can't be the best we can without family...
We can't be the best we can without schools...
We can't be the best we can without the skills of others...
We can't be the best we can without talking and understanding each other...
And you have been failing at that...
Do you hear me?

He goes to her and embraces her.
After a moment of quiet… they start to sway lightly in each other's arms.

**Melania** — You have to find and harness the strength of the group… not simply the strength of a part of it.

They pull apart as they face each other and hold hands.

**Donald** — You don't think I'm being treated unfairly?
**Melania** — I do not. The Mueller probe is an effort to preserve the nation… you need to respect that.
**Donald** — I didn't collude… but maybe… Russia's interference did throw the election my way.

She looks at him.

**Donald** — I have to allow for that possibility.
**Melania** — Did you obstruct justice?
**Donald** — I did not.

She closes her eyes for a moment.

**Melania** — If you could say that in public…
**Donald** — I've been saying that I didn't collude…
**Melania** — No, the part about you now believing that Russian interference did influence the election in your favor… and that if not, maybe Hillary would've been elected.
**Donald** — What difference would that make?
**Melania** — A huge difference.
**Donald** — Even if it can't be proved?
**Melania** — Even so.

Just that statement would give the nation a sense that we prize fairness… and that you as our leader, values it most of all… and it would remind us all of how egregious has been the action of another nation to violate our sovereignty… and how we must pull together to defend ourselves and our way of life… and impose whatever sanctions are needed to put an immediate halt to that kind of behavior.

**Donald** — But I would be putting my legitimacy in question…

**Melania** — Your legitimacy has been in question… but in the absence of proof you could not be removed from office… and you would have the rest of your term to work to strengthen us as a nation.

**Donald** — It would raise the likelihood of impeachment…

**Melania** — Not if you have nothing to hide.

**Donald** — They could come up with fake evidence…

**Melania** — That's your paranoia talking. You have to check that. In the end… if impeachment comes… you have to trust that your own sense of fairness will be repaid.

He shakes his head slowly.

**Donald** — I'm not as trusting as you are.
**Melania** — I'll stand by you.

She takes him by the hand and they walk off toward the White House.

# 12

Moscow. Putin's dacha. Afternoon.

Putin is outside with his dog, standing on a little hill by the lake.

**Putin** — Why do I do it?
For the pleasure of it.
The pleasure of seeing the dominant nation in the world, being tossed about by our actions.
The pleasure of seeing them go at each other... doubting, hating, reviling each other...

He laughs.

The supposedly dominant nation in the world... electing whom they elected... hating immigrants when they are a nation of immigrants... questioning their values... what is there not to like about that?

He smiles to himself, picks up a stone and throws it far off and into the lake. His dog gives a start at his side but Putin calms him down.

The more confusion I stir in that land, the weaker their resolve to block any move I make to extend my influence or my territory.
I on this side, Xi Jinping on the other. Both enlarging our spheres of influence.
And the more divided the Americans, the more China will continue to insert itself in Latin America... right in their

backyard. And in Africa, too.
Meanwhile, I strengthen my support for Far Right movements in Italy, Hungary, Poland, even Germany.
Let the Americans bicker with the Europeans… the more distracted, the better.

He laughs.

I have time. Oh, the virtues of autocracy. One nation, one man.

He pets his dog.

Do I need to do it?
Out of a sense of self-preservation? Yes.
But there's also the satisfaction of having control over the lives of other men and women.
Men and women who live under the delusion that they are free.

He kneels down to speak to his dog.

Right?

The dog licks Putin's hand.

Because he made money in his hotels he thinks he can be a leader… ha!

The dog makes an affectionate sound.

Putin stands again.

But we'll see, for sure, once I get his tax returns.
Still… there's that virus that could spread here… or anywhere…
The virus of wanting an open dialogue… the virus of freedom…
freedom to criticize… to question authority… to make money… to be all you can be… to dare climb the ladder… no… I will not have that here in Russia.
But I'm not really worried.
After all… we're the land of the Czars… of Stalin…
of institutionalized cruelty… the mass killing of dissidents…
Russians killing Russians…
by the millions…
We have a long way to go to heal those wounds… if ever…
America has never experienced such abuse as Russians endured…
Except for black Americans.
But nothing… nothing like we have.

He turns to his dog.

Our cyber warriors will take care of things, won't they, Washington?
So we can even out the playing field.

The dog makes a wimpy sound.

I need to get you something to eat.

The two start walking down the little hill toward the dacha.

In the distance, guards in black garb are posted at various locations.

# 13

A very dark, rectangular room, barely lit, and Donald sitting at one end.
The same shadowy figure with no discernible features, a black suit and a hood over his head, appears at the other end.
As before, at the wave of the Man's hand a chair materializes and he sits facing Donald.

**Donald** — You again?

The Man nods slowly.

**Man** — You're running out of time. The mid terms are coming up... and the democrats are gaining... so unless Mueller clears you... they will likely move to impeach you.
**Donald** — On what grounds?
**Man** — Mueller is scaring some folks.
**Donald** — Their word against mine. Can you be more specific?
**Man** — Cannot. But you're the big fish...
**Donald** — And a good incentive for someone to flip. I know that.
I'm not worried, though. We'll keep the house and the senate. I'm sure about that.

The Man leans forward, arms on his legs.

**Donald** — Say, how come I can't see your face?
**Man** — I don't have one.

Donald squirms.

**Man** — What mistake did you make?
**Donald** — Mistake?

Donald looks down at the ground, searchingly.

**Man** — If you know, you may still have a chance…

A moment passes. Donald looks up at the Man, still unable to come up with an answer.

**Man** — Don't know?
**Donald** — Melania… she's talked about the need for dialogue…

The Man nods slowly.

**Donald** — … building bridges…

The Man nods again.

**Donald** — Finding my higher… self…
**Man** — … and?
**Donald** — I don't think it's in me.
**Man** — I see.
**Donald** — What do you see?
**Man** — Really want my opinion?
**Donald** — I don't know… I suppose…
**Man** — There may not be enough time… but here it goes…

Donald sits back, bracing himself, wary of the Man's answer.

**Man** — You played the one note... and that's all.
**Donald** — The one note?
**Man** — Same note... again and again... you got lucky that the one note attracted a lot of customers at the start... but you got stuck on it... and here you are, well into your second year, and you're still on the same note.
**Donald (puzzled)** — One note...
**Man** — You need more than one note to find your depth as a leader.

Donald hangs his head for a moment.

**Donald (quickly, anxiously)** — One note... two notes... three notes... what difference does it make? I keep my promises.
**Man (calmly)** — The thing is... leading is about much more than that.
**Donald** — More than keeping your promises?

The Man slowly reaches forward with his long right arm, and keeping it extended then turns the palm of his hand upward. Donald draws back.

**Man** — Touch the soul...

Donald is tempted to reach out and touch the Man's hand but is afraid of it.

**Donald** — Touch the soul? The soul? Ha! Look, I've made a lot of decisions in my year and a half...
**Man** — ... but have you led...?

Donald is disconcerted.

**Donald (timidly)** — No?

The Man shakes his head very slowly.

**Donald (rousing himself)** — What about the stock market, it's going up and up, and the GDP, the tax cut, and the low unemployment... I'm giving people what they want... money... money! Isn't that what we're all about... the rest just empty pieties?

Donald lets out a loud laugh, but the Man doesn't stir, all the while keeping his arm extended, the palm facing up. A somber expression then settles on Donald... fearful that he's missing out on something but unable to overcome his fear.

**Donald (not giving up, rousing himself again)** — Remember Liza and Joel in Cabaret... the movie? Money Money Money! Makes the world go round!

The Man then lowers his head and pulls back his arm.

**Donald** — What's the matter with you, you don't watch the movies... you too good for them?

Donald stands up abruptly and is surprised he is able to do it.

**Donald (looking at his wrists)** — Hunh... I thought I'd be held back... like the first time... how come I can move now?

The Man stands up.

Donald takes a few determined steps toward the Man but then stops. They look at each other in silence for a moment.

**Donald (softly, tentatively)** — You think I have it in me?

The Man pauses, then turns and starts to walk off.

**Donald** — Hey, wait a minute, I asked you a question!

Donald lunges for the Man but the figure disappears and Donald ends up falling to the ground.
Slowly, he sits up and looks around at the dark, empty room. The Man's chair is still there.
Donald gets up and approaches it carefully. He sits on it.

Now he hears the disembodied voice of the Man.

**Man** — One note.

Donald covers his ears for a moment… frightened.
All is still.
He lowers his hands slowly… then… seized by a fit of rage, jumps to his feet.

**Donald (shouting full blast)** — God dammit! I said god dammit! Do you hear me?
God dammit! The hell with everybody! God dammit! Yes, you, god… damn you!!

**Man** — One note.

Donald drops to his knees… head bowed… and starts to cry softly.

A moment passes.
Then he begins to raise his head… as tears stream down his face…
and while slowly extending his arms upwards… cries out…

**Donald (pleadingly, anguished)** — Can't I have depth? Can't I…? Please god… give me depth!

White House. Bedroom. 2 am.

Donald wakes up with a startle.
Melania is asleep at his side.
He rubs his face. Then gets up and crosses to the window, opens the drapes and pulls up a chair. He sits and looks out into the night.

Melania awakens. She looks at him.

**Melania** — What happened?

He shrugs.

**Melania** — Another dream?

He nods.

**Melania** — Want to talk about it?

He says nothing.
She rises and goes to his side and stands behind him as she begins to rub his shoulders.

**Donald** — I have to make some decisions.

She kisses the crown of his head.

**Melania** — Just know that I love you.

# 14

Oval Office. 3 am.

Donald is alone at his desk, staring off.
He raises his hands to his temples… then he begins…

To all the women whom I have mistreated… I beg your forgiveness… in my fits of narcissism I violated your boundaries… treated you like chattel… thought myself entitled to your bodies to satisfy my carnal desires. Owning up to my transgressions is an acknowledgment of the predator impulse in me… a first step to understand it and to control it… for I have caused emotional injuries that have left you with scars. I have no doubt that… with the assistance of my wife Melania… I will in time conquer that disgraceful flaw in my character… and help me move toward becoming a better human being… and a better man.

He swivels in his chair to face the window that looks out onto the city.

I've memorized my culpability speech… but will I ever make it public?

He leans forward, hands clasped, the mood pensive.

Melania would say that it's the right thing to do.

He stands up.

Will I be mocked?

I can see women saying, 'it's too late'… questioning my sincerity.
Some will try to take me to court but, without any physical evidence, I should be okay.
What worries me is what my base will say.
They accept me as who I am. A manly guy who loves…
But that's in the past. I'm giving it up. For Melania.

He turns to walk into the room, hands held in back.

What will the political fallout be?
This finding my higher self… and my emotional depth… has political risks.
And then Melania wanting me to be a bipartisan President.

He stops.

I'm not saying it's not possible but it's a stretch.
Still… I have to find that sweet spot in me from where to draw the strength to confront Putin. And I have to find it now.
Could it be… that making my culpability speech public… will take me to where I have to go?

He sits by the fireplace.

Something about owning up to the truth as a source of psychological strength.
What would I say to Putin?

He pauses, then narrowing his eyes leans forward and begins to speak to the imaginary Putin.

Look man… whatever you have on me, you have on me. I
don't care what it is.
I do not care. If you helped me get elected, so be it.
That's right.
I owe allegiance to my country, got that?
That's right.
I owe allegiance to my people… that means everybody.
Native and immigrant. White, black and brown and
whatever lies in between. Protestant and Catholic, Jew and
Muslim.
And yes, I've taken a vow to protect and nurture the
American mind.
With whatever wrinkles it may have.
So here's the deal, Vladimir…
You have to stop interfering in my country's elections… or in
anything else.
Did you get that?
By hook or crook, it has fallen to me, a hotel businessman
from New York,
That great city who survived 9/11,
To protect and enhance the American way of life,
With all its defects,
Because we keep learning, buster, did you get that?
We keep learning so we can make it better,
And if you do not stop,
Then I will start piling up sanctions on you,
One after the other, until your people are sick of them.
And once they get to that point they'll come to you and say,
'what's the deal, Vladimir?'
'are you representing us or are you on a power trip?'
because we're the ones getting hurt with the sanctions, not
you.'

He sits back in his chair.

What did you say?

He leans forward again.

That your interference in the election was vaster than it's known?
Okay. Then put it out, man. Just put it out.
You can't prove anything.
You do not control the American mind.
Period. Okay?
That's your delusion.
And you do not control my mind.
No one does.
I am now putting an end to the nightmares, all right?
Do you understand?
I am in control of my mind.
That's it. Case Closed. Dismissed.

He nods and sits back.

I like that. It felt good.

He crosses his legs. More relaxed.

You are not Russia, Vladimir, like I am not America. Our nations are greater than us.
Better than us. Smarter than us.
And if you don't stop your cyber warriors, I'm warning you, I will punish you with sanctions till your people are hurting so bad they'll tell you to go to hell.

He smiles to himself.

I should've said something like that in Helsinki.
But I didn't.
Okay. We get to have second chances in this country. And third ones.
I'm taking mine.

He stands.

Wow. I feel lighter. This feels good. Melania had a point.

He stretches his arms over his head.

I feel great, beautiful. Yes! I liked that part about our countries being better and smarter than us. It just came out. Love it.

He walks back to the window, looks out.

Wow. Feeling the way I am… I might just… what?

A thought occurs to him that takes him by surprise. He is astonished.

Really? I'll be darned. Who would've thought? I should tell Melania.
She's probably asleep, though.
But I'll wake her up, she won't mind.
No, it can wait.
No… it shouldn't wait.

He crosses to the door to exit but stops. He turns around and looks in the direction of the Andrew Jackson portrait. He walks over and stands before it.

Stonewall… I wanted to tell you… right here, today… and God is my witness…
That I'm taking a vow to protect and nurture the American Soul.

Jackson smiles at him.

Thank you, buddy.

He returns to the door and exits the office.

# 15

White House. Bedroom suite. 4 am.

Melania is at the table writing on her journal.

Donald enters.

**Donald** — Hey. How come you're up?
**Melania** — Wanted to wait for you.
**Donald** — That's sweet.

He goes to her and kisses her. He pulls up a chair and sits opposite her.

**Melania** — Something's on your mind.
**Donald** — Yes… I was talking to Putin…
**Melania** — This early…?
**Donald** — The imaginary Putin…

She is intrigued.

**Donald** — … and I told him he had to stop the interference. Period.
**Melania** — Okay. You're practicing…
**Donald** — It's done. I'm going to do it.
**Melania (surprised)** — I need to hear this…
**Donald** — You will. Tonight, for sure. I want to go over it again. But that's not what I wanted to tell you.

He takes her hands in his.

**Donald** — What I wanted to tell you was that it felt great telling Putin to back off or else. I don't care what he has on me. And feeling great… I had this thought that I wanted to share with you.
**Melania** — What?
**Donald** — You won't believe it.
**Melania** — The suspense grows…
**Donald** — Feeling as good as I felt from my conversation with Putin… I realized…
**Melania** — Yes…?
**Donald** (**smiling proudly**) — That we don't have to build the Wall.

Melania gives a gasp.

**Melania** — Are you serious?
**Donald** — Yes. I'm going to walk it back.
**Melania** — Oh, my god.
**Donald** — It was a ripple effect from my imaginary talk with Putin.
I realized, that I could come out as a leader… and that doing so meant telling my base that… after careful consideration…. those moneys would be better spent in programs for their education and training to acquire new skills… to help them become a cutting edge workforce… and that I still would be keeping my commitment to stopping illegal immigration… but that considering all costs and our existing border guards… building a Wall was unnecessary.
**Melania** (**joyously**) — I knew you could surprise me!

She leans over and embraces him.

**Donald** — I realize it would be a test for my base. They

have believed in me. But it's the right thing to do.

Tears have welled up in Melania's eyes. She dabs them dry.

**Melania** — I thought this moment would never come.
**Donald** — I know... I didn't either... it surprised me.

She pulls back slightly.

**Melania** — And the Mueller investigation?
**Donald** — I will endorse it as the right thing to do... for the good of the nation... a nation that is better and smarter than I am.
**Melania** — No more witch hunt?
**Donald** — No more witch hunt.

She still doesn't believe it.

He gets up, takes a few steps into the room and, going down on one knee, lets himself drop to the ground, to lie flat and face the ceiling.

**Melania** — Please tell me that this isn't a joke?
**Donald** — It's not a joke.
**Melania** — How did this happen?

She goes to him and lies on the ground next to him.

**Donald** — It was the nightmares... I felt so humiliated by them... and I knew I had to push back.

He takes her hand in his.

**Donald** — You know what this means, don't you?
**Melania** — What?
**Donald** — My base may not be supportive... they may not go along with me... they may feel betrayed... and I may not be nominated in 2020... if I survive the Mueller probe. But I have to do the right thing... or I'll be running scared and in shame for the rest of my life.
**Melania** — I love you.

They turn to face each other, while still on the ground.

**Melania** — When are you going to tell Putin...?
**Donald** — Tomorrow. And then I'll hold a press conference.
**Melania** — Does anybody else know?
**Donald** — Just you. It will be a surprise. I won't tell anybody in advance.
I will then fully endorse the importance of the Mueller probe.
**Melania** — What do you think the party will say?
**Donald** — I don't care. For some things, I don't consult the party. I'm not a committee.

She gently caresses his face.

**Melania** — Have you thought of apologizing to women?
**Donald** — I have... I've memorized that short speech you heard a while back... but I want to wait a few days before I go public. But I promise I will.

They kiss... and make love.

# 16

Two days later.

NY Times headline.

## President Trump Takes Charge.

In a surprise press conference, the President admits to the nation that Russian hacking may have played a decisive role in his election. He then proceeded to give his full endorsement to the Mueller probe. He provided the details of a phone conversation with Mr Putin, held earlier in the day, demanding an immediate stop to any interference with the American electoral process. Speculation has run rampant regarding the motives for the President's about face…

The following day

Washington Post headline.

## President Trump Says Bye Bye to the Wall.

While remaining committed to immigration reform, the President announced that he would not include building the wall as a priority. "We can use the money for education and training of the American work force," he said to a stunned crowd at a rally in West Virginia. But there were no boos in the arena…
Pundits were left puzzled at the move, with some speculating that he is feeling more secure as we head into the mid—term elections… with others seeing it as an effort to broaden his support and woo the center…

The decision comes right after taking an unexpected tough stance against Russian interference and openly stating that had it not been for the interference, Hillary Clinton may well have been elected President…

The stock market greeted the news with relish and the Dow jumped 581 points to an all time high…

# 17

Washington DC. Park. Evening.

Two men in suits approach. They spot a bench and sit side by side. They pull out their cell phones, turn them off and place them on the bench between them.

**1st** — Pretty crazy.
**2nd** — We knew he was full of surprises.
**1st** — It's insane. After all we've done to provide him with cover.
**2nd** — I know. He must think we're a yo—yo.
**1st** — You think the base will go with him?
**2nd** — They have a love affair with this guy… I don't see it.
**1st** — But there it is.
What bugs me is his new talk about bipartisan dialogue, where did that come from?
**2nd** — You vote for him?
**1st** — Holding my nose.
**2nd** — We all did.
**1st** — Well, they can't prove anything so we'll keep our seats.
**2nd** — Maybe he had a stroke… one of those silent ones…
**1st** — Anything is possible.
**2nd** — Maybe he got hit by lightning… I read about this doctor who got hit during a rainstorm and became a pianist afterwards… he hadn't been musical before.
**1st** — No kidding. I suppose it could go the other way… and become a dope fiend.
I'll tell you this… if he gets the base to stay with him… that's the rabbit out of the hat trick.
**2nd** — If he does that… he'll win the next election.

**1st** — Bipartisan dialogue… can you believe it? We haven't done that in so long we don't know what it sounds like.
**2nd** — On the other hand… maybe we'll get something done for a change.
**1st** — I suppose so.
I'm up for reelection and my opponent is getting all kinds of donations. Women and immigrants are up in arms.
**2nd** — You worried?
**1st** — A little.

They look at each other.

**2nd** — I'll hate to miss our chats.
**1st** — Don't count me out, yet.

A gay couple goes by. They're holding hands as they talk amorously.

# 18

White House. One week later.

Press Conference. Late Afternoon.

The President at the lectern, Melania standing near him on one side, Ivanka on the other.

**Donald** — To all the women whom I have mistreated… I beg your forgiveness… in my fits of narcissism I violated your boundaries… treated you like chattel… thought myself entitled to your bodies to satisfy my carnal desires. Owning up to my transgressions is an acknowledgment of the predator impulse in me… a first step to understand it and to control it… for I have caused emotional injuries that have left you with scars. I have no doubt that… with the assistance of my wife Melania… I will in time conquer that disgraceful flaw in my character… and help me move toward becoming a better human being… and a better man.
Thank you.

Reporters jump to their feet with an abundance of questions but the President simply waves to them and exits.

# 19

White House. South Lawn. Midday.

Melania is strolling on her own.
Donald comes into the garden and calls to her.

**Donald** — Melania!

She waves back at him
He approaches and they embrace.

**Donald** — What did you think?
**Melania** — It went very well.
**Donald** — I thought so, too. Will it help us win the election?
**Melania** — Dee… what will be will be… and we'll always have each other.

They turn and holding hands, start to walk off.
After a stretch…

**Melania** — Have you thought about the tax returns?
**Donald** — Ah, those… let me think about that one some more.


The End

This is a dramatization of events. I do not know Mr Trump, Melania or Mr Putin.

Thanks to the American press, Right, Left and Center.

I am a self published author. Your posting a review of this work is much appreciated. Thanks.

CPSIA information can be obtained
at www.ICGtesting.com
Printed in the USA
FSHW01n1716250918
52476FS